Grow It Back!

Diana Noonan

Contents

Hair

If you cut
your hair ...

it will grow
back!

Tail

Animals can grow things back, too!
A bird pecks a lizard's tail.
The tail comes off.

The lizard runs away.
The tail will grow back.

Here is the new tail.

Arm

A bird picks up a starfish.

The arm of the starfish comes off.
It will grow back.

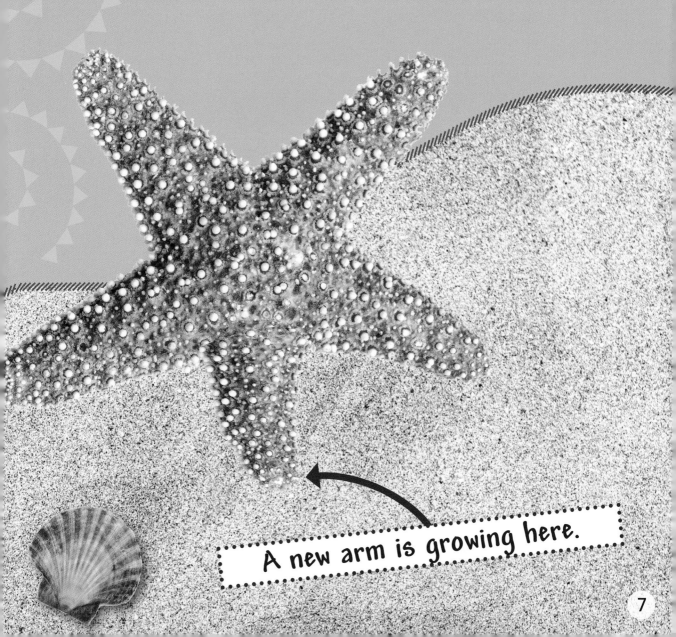

A new arm is growing here.

Leg

A bird pecks a stick insect's leg.

The leg comes off, but it will grow back.

A new leg is growing here.

Claw

A bird pecks at a crab's claw.
The claw comes off.

Missing claw

The claw will grow back.

Here is the new claw.

Antlers

The deer have a fight with their antlers.

antlers

An antler comes off, but it will grow back.

A new antler is growing here.

Teeth

A shark has lots of teeth.
They can come out, but
they will grow back.

You have lots of little teeth. When they come out, you will grow new teeth!

Index